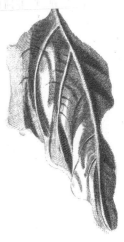

Good Morning Poems

"George Bowering's title *Good Morning Poems*, can be variously read — as a greeting to historic poems, as poems from centuries-ago mornings that are 'good,' and as poems that welcome you to today. These seem to be poems which have been welcoming Bowering for quite a while, from 'Back in the mists of time when I was a university English student.' Yet overall his selections and one-page commentaries approach current expectations for race and gender diversity — one of numerous surprises he can find for us in these still welcoming lyrics."

FRANK DAVEY, award-winning author of *Poems Suitable to Current Material Conditions* and *aka bpNichol: a preliminary biography*

"I am not a morning person. I am, though, a George Bowering person — and this neat little book gives readers access not only to Bowering the writer, but to George the mentor, teacher, and language-drunk friend, dizzy with all the possibilities of words, phrases, sentences, images, allusions, metaphors, assonances, and rhymes. Here he is in all of his infectious enthusiasm for some of the finest poetry ever written in English. I can't imagine a better guide."

CHARLES DEMERS, author of *Property Values*

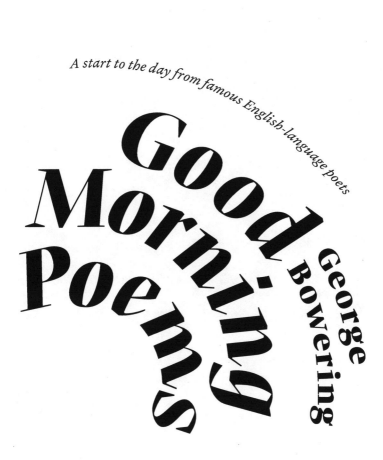

A start to the day from famous English-language poets

Good Morning Poems

George Bowering

NeWest Press

Library and Archives Canada Cataloguing in Publication
Title: Good morning poems : a start to the day from famous English-language poets / George Bowering.
Names: Bowering, George, 1935– editor.
Identifiers: Canadiana (print) 20220402299 | Canadiana (ebook) 2022040237X | ISBN 9781774390658 (softcover) | ISBN 9781774390665 (EPUB)
Subjects: LCSH: English poetry. | LCSH: American poetry.
Classification: LCC PR1175 .G66 2023 | DDC 821.008—DC23

NeWest Press wishes to acknowledge that the land on which we operate is Treaty 6 territory and a traditional meeting ground and home for many Indigenous Peoples, including Cree, Saulteaux, Niitsitapi (Blackfoot), Métis, and Nakota Sioux.

Editor for the Press: Leslie Vermeer
Cover and interior design: Natalie Olsen
Cover image: Asar Studios / Alamy Stock Photo
Author photo: Kris Krug, https://kriskrug.co/

This is a work of literary criticism and any quotations within are used as such.

NeWest Press acknowledges the support of the Canada Council for the Arts, the Alberta Foundation for the Arts, and the Edmonton Arts Council for support of our publishing program. We acknowledge the financial support of the Government of Canada through the Canada Book Fund for our publishing activities.

NeWest Press
#201, 8540-109 Street
Edmonton, Alberta T6G 1E6
www.newestpress.com

No bison were harmed in the making of this book.
Printed and bound in Canada

For Douglas and Sharon Barbour

Contents

AFTERWORD: How to Enjoy a Good Evening Poem

Preface

First Thing in the Morning

The older I get, the more things I have to do first thing in the morning. You know, exercises, face washing, eye drops, air puffer, pills, hearing aids and so forth. It takes nearly an hour to get to cereal and banana and coffee. These are all things I have to do before I get to do what I want to do — which is to read a poem. Morning is the best time to read a poem. One morning it might be some lines by Christopher Marlowe. Next morning it could be the new volume from Nicole Brossard — in French or English. Often I will go page by page through a new edition of a book by one of my friends. But if you are going to read a poem to welcome your day, it seems to me best to choose something you've read before, either a return to something you could not quite follow some decades earlier or a poem you've read so often that you just about have it by heart.

Some people like to go for a walk in the woods or to the coffee shop in the morning. Some poets have even written poems about morning walks. I'm not that extreme — I'll settle for a chair at the table, a cup of dark coffee, and a page or two of Denise Levertov. Lots of poets have written to or about the early hours, which suggests that if you are working on the *New York Times* crossword and thus have a pen in your hand, it might be as pleasant to write a poem as to read one. I'd just as soon read a poem, though, say "January Morning" by William Carlos Williams, any month of the year. Maybe my morning poem routine began before my morning coffee did. When I was a boy I had a series of books entitled *Junior Classics*, ten volumes from Collier. The books were colour coded, with Volume 10 being pink for poems. I eventually let my sister keep the other nine books and kept this one, which is now a hundred years old. There are many forgettable poems and forgotten poets in it, but that is where I first found Shelley's skylark and Goldsmith's deserted village, and the north wind that blew Anonymous my way.

I guess I've always wanted to put together a collection of the poems I like. It's likely that lots of people, whether they read poems in the morning or not, would like to make such an anthology. Maybe some of them think that it would be interesting to make a few remarks to or about the poems and put them across the page from each one. I know I did, and here they are. I hope that readers might like to offer their own responses — to the poems or to the other pages.

Good Morning Poems

Sir Thomas Wyatt (1503–1542)

They Flee from Me

They flee from me that sometime did me seek
With naked foot, stalking in my chamber.
I have seen them gentle, tame, and meek,
That now are wild and do not remember
That sometime they put themself in danger
To take bread at my hand; and now they range,
Busily seeking with a continual change.

Thanked be fortune it hath been otherwise
Twenty times better; but once in special,
In thin array after a pleasant guise,
When her loose gown from her shoulders did fall,
And she me caught in her arms long and small;
Therewithall sweetly did me kiss
And softly said, "Dear heart, how like you this?"

It was no dream: I lay broad waking.
But all is turned thorough my gentleness
Into a strange fashion of forsaking;
And I have leave to go of her goodness,
And she also, to use newfangleness.
But since that I so kindly am served
I would fain know what she hath deserved.

I was for years snagged and delighted by the difficulty of this poem and wondered how much of that difficulty was created by the half-millennium that has flowed over the language since it was composed. It was my first wife's favourite old poem, and I know she discussed it at length with Rob Dunham, a superb poetry reader back in the day. Wyatt liked complicated verse forms, as he introduced Italy's sonnet to Britain, and composed "They Flee from Me" in rhyme royale, which was probably Chaucer's invention, his variation on some European rime schemes. I decided to go at the poem not from the beginning, not toward the close, but right into the core. The very centre is the line "When her loose gown from her shoulders did fall." I am an old codger, but that image still gets me stirring. The line is also the centre of the second stanza. The first stanza introduces regret. The third stanza brings resentment and sarcasm. The poor old guy: first there were all these young things sneaking into his bedroom; then there was the special one that turned him from Lothario to poet in love; now there is bitterness that shows us how a poem can be ruined by a gripe. What a successful feat by Wyatt, to wreck his poem in order to make it work! Yes, the poem's argument is introduced in the first line, and we seem to be in for a regular poetical complaint, but then the complaint grows a little ugly as the plural gives way to the singular and then something less than that. And Thomas Wyatt was still in his thirties when he died.

Queen Elizabeth I (1533–1603)

On Monsieur's Departure

I grieve and dare not show my discontent,
I love and yet am forced to seem to hate,
I do, yet dare not say I ever meant,
I seem stark mute but inwardly do prate.
I am and not, I freeze and yet am burned,
Since from myself another self I turned.

My care is like my shadow in the sun,
Follows me flying, flies when I pursue it,
Stands and lies by me, doth what I have done.
His too familiar care doth make me rue it.
No means I find to rid him from my breast,
Till by the end of things it be supprest.

Some gentler passion slide into my mind,
For I am soft and made of melting snow;
Or be more cruel, love, and so be kind.
Let me or float or sink, be high or low.
Or let me live with some more sweet content,
Or die and so forget what love ere meant.

Imagine having your name given to the era often called the greatest in English poetry. Surely that makes up for being a poet less gifted or accomplished than so many of your subjects. Elizabeth dodged the axes and evil looks of many well-dressed men, and somehow received an education equal to most of theirs. She did a lot of writing, most of it speeches and official letters, plus a few poems scratched on windows and penned on royal walls. She read her courtiers' poems and tried to imitate their tricks and, as in her prose, strove for special effects. If you want to describe her versification, check what she is wearing in her many painted portraits, the pro-liferate ruffles and gems and cosmetics — call it decoration as style. "On Monsieur's Departure," whoever the monsieur may have been, is that most common of Elizabethan exer-cises, a poet/lover's complaint. There are three stanzas that are really three Shakespearean sonnet sestets, or perhaps rhyme royale stanzas with the fifth lines removed. In either case, the first five lines of the poem begin with the word "I", and first-person pronouns abound throughout. This reader harbours no doubt that the "virgin" queen suffered enough to make such a complaint. Yes, most of the language and vision is pretty stiff and otherwise amateurish, but the poet can sing, as she does in lines two and three of the middle stanza — before she wrecks it all with a stupid rime at the end of line four.

Sir Philip Sidney (1554–1586)

Sonnet 31 [from *Astrophil and Stella*]

With how sad steps, O Moon, thou climb'st the skies!
How silently, and with how wan a face!
What! may it be that even in heavenly place
That busy archer his sharp arrows tries?
Sure, if that long-with-love-acquainted eyes
Can judge of love, thou feel'st a lover's case:
I read it in thy looks; thy languished grace
To me, that feel the like, thy state descries.
Then, even of fellowship, O Moon, tell me,
Is constant love deemed there but want of wit?
Are beauties there as proud as here they be?
Do they above love to be loved, and yet
Those lovers scorn whom that love doth possess?
Do they call 'virtue' there — ungratefulness?

When I was a young university student in Vancouver I fell for this poem, and though I am not very good at memorizing, I have never forgotten its first two lines. I spoke them aloud one winter's night in Calgary when I was a young English professor, walking between buildings at the university and looking up at the full moon. It's the thirty-first sonnet in Sidney's *Astrophil and Stella*, usually considered the first great sonnet sequence in English and published in the 1580s. The poem borrows Petrarch's Italian scansion, and it continues the ancient association between poets and the moon; so people who have read a fair bit of poetry, then or now, suspect that Sidney might have been having a little fun with the moony speaker of these lines. If we start with the first poem in the sequence, it may become hard to recite them without flailing one's arms. Who could blame us when we all know that the speaker is stuck on a woman whose name means "star," especially given that his own name means "star-lover"? In the octave Astrophil(ip) here sees a likeness between the moon's apparent lovesickness and his own, then uses the sestet to voice a traditional lover's complaint (Shakespeare's the most famous). But is Sidney performing a lovely poem in a tradition, or gently satirizing the complainant with whom he identifies? I don't think that there is anything wrong with holding to both possibilities. Look at the phrase "That busy archer." It looks as if the poet (Philip or Astrophil) is gently insulting Cupid out of resentment and thus showing himself to be a long way from heroic. Meanwhile, isn't this a beautiful poem?

William Shakespeare (1564–1616)

Sonnet 55

Not marble nor the gilded monuments
Of princes shall outlive this powerful rhyme,
But you shall shine more bright in these contents
Than unswept stone besmeared with sluttish time.
When wasteful war shall statues overturn,
And broils root out the work of masonry,
Nor Mars his sword nor war's quick fire shall burn
The living record of your memory.
'Gainst death and all-oblivious enmity
Shall you pace forth; your praise shall still find room
Even in the eyes of all posterity
That wear this world out to the ending doom.
So, till the Judgement that yourself arise,
You live in this, and dwell in lovers' eyes.

A main purpose of the blues, or its less musical offspring, hip-hop, is riming boastfulness, with all its humorous effrontery. Howlin' Wolf may have been "three hundred pounds of heavenly joy," and the Notorious B.I.G. thought he was something with "all my n—s, all my guns, all my women," but William Shakespeare got a head start four hundred years earlier and is not likely to be overtaken anytime soon if ever. He had the advantage in talent and intelligence. The conventional reading is that "Sonnet 55" was in a sequence addressed to a mysterious youth, but it doesn't take much more than a glance to see that the poet was thinking of his readers far in the future. The poet's boast is that this poetic monument (a word whose root meaning is memory) will itself be alive when even stone memorials have gone, while the world is wearing away. So "you" will be living, let's say, four centuries from now — and he has delivered on his boast. Most formerly gilded monuments are now bereft of their gold, and most are already Ozymandiases on the ground. This poem about this poem, though, partakes of spirit; it is made of breath and hence lives while life does. If fire, the creative/destructive element, could incinerate every printed record of the poem, the poem would survive, and thus so would the commemorated one. Shakespeare's ear is the horn of the immortal: "Mars" rimes with "war's," and ironically such music will sing the subject alive — "You live in this." This poet resembles the creator in Genesis, doesn't he?

Thomas Campion (1567–1620)

My Sweetest Lesbia

My sweetest Lesbia, let us live and love,
And though the sager sort our deeds reprove,
Let us not weigh them. Heaven's great lamps do dive
Into their west, and straight again revive,
But soon as once set is our little light,
Then must we sleep one ever-during night.

If all would lead their lives in love like me,
Then bloody swords and armor should not be;
No drum nor trumpet peaceful sleeps should move,
Unless alarm came from the camp of love.
But fools do live, and waste their little light,
And seek with pain their ever-during night.

When timely death my life and fortune ends,
Let not my hearse be vexed with mourning friends,
But let all lovers, rich in triumph, come
And with sweet pastimes grace my happy tomb;
And Lesbia, close up thou my little light,
And crown with love my ever-during night.

Take a look at that first line, by which I mean have a listen to it. Just about everything rimes with the lady's assigned name. "Lesbia" is immediately almost repeated in "let us." Then the liquids pour through the poem: "live and love," followed by "let us" again, leading to "little light," poking its nose up in "sleep." The first line of the second sestet will also boast five occasions — "all" and "lead" and "lives like." Well, you can count the rest of the ell letters. It's like a love lullaby, which makes music, while every stanza leads to everlasting night after death. You would not be surprised to hear that Campion, after attending Cambridge, then going to law school, then to medical school, later serving the army in battle, became a composer. Most of his poems are the words of songs, and he is usually paired with his contemporary Shakespeare as the most musical of Elizabethan–Jacobean poets. All lyric poems should be spoken aloud, of course, and readers will learn in this way that Campion is simply most musical. "My Sweetest Lesbia" begins as an English version of Catullus's fervid love verse to *his* sweet Lesbia, but soon exceeds the Roman poem in complexity and beauty. If you read twentieth-century U.S. poet Robert Creeley's early poems, you will see (hear) why he liked Campion so much.

John Donne (1572–1631)

Holy Sonnet XIV

Batter my heart, three-person'd God, for you
As yet but knock, breathe, shine, and seek to mend;
That I may rise and stand, o'erthrow me, and bend
Your force to break, blow, burn, and make me new.
I, like an usurp'd town to'another due,
Labor to admit you, but oh, to no end;
Reason, your viceroy in me, me should defend,
But is captiv'd, and proves weak or untrue.
Yet dearly I love you, and would be lov'd fain,
But am betroth'd unto your enemy;
Divorce me, untie or break that knot again,
Take me to you, imprison me, for I,
Except you enthrall me, never shall be free,
Nor ever chaste, except you ravish me.

Back in the mists of time, when I was a university English student, our U.S. literature professor scoffed at our suggestion that Walt Whitman's poems may have been about homosexual desire. In that same year our Elizabethan literature professor resisted our notion that Donne's "Holy Sonnet XIV" resembled an invitation to a rapist Jehovah. Donne's poetry often portrayed its author as celebrating physical love, though in the last of his many occupations, as an ex-Catholic Anglican cleric, he might be expected to soft-pedal the subject. Yes, Donne's great sequence is called *Holy Sonnets*, but we do remember that the Italians invented sonnets as love songs. Donne, never a gradualist, begins his poem with "Batter my heart," and ends with "ravish me." Innocent present-day readers may not like the association of such sexual violence with their "three-person'd God," but a lot of simple folk, especially in the U.S., believe in something they call "the rapture," whereby God grabs pre-chosen airline pilots or running backs during their working hours and yanks them up to Heaven. As for ravishing, check a Keats ode in which a "still unravished bride" appears (Keats, like Donne, was nuts about paradox). Long before those two poems, King Solomon wrote some sexy poems addressed to one or more of his many brides and mistresses. But even he did not take as many as Jesus did — you know that nuns are brides of Christ. They understand Donne's clever words: "Take me to you, imprison me, for I / Except you enthrall me, never shall be free." There are chattel and cattle, finger rings and nose rings. Living property.

Ben Jonson (1572–1637)

Still to Be Neat, Still to Be Dressed

Still to be neat, still to be dressed,
As you were going to a feast;
Still to be powdered, still perfumed;
Lady, it is to be presumed,
Though art's hid causes are not found,
All is not sweet, all is not sound.

Give me a look, give me a face,
That makes simplicity a grace;
Robes loosely flowing, hair as free;
Such sweet neglect more taketh me
Than all th' adulteries of art.
They strike mine eyes, but not my heart.

Here, Ben Jonson taps into one of the standard themes of lyric and satirical poetry since the days of the Romans — a declaration in favour of simplicity in the arts and other products of the human imagination and taste. At the beginning of the seventeenth century, in fact, poets who favoured classical verse and plain English were called the "sons of Ben." Robert Herrick's "Delight in Disorder" was inspired by Jonson's "Such sweet neglect." William Carlos Williams, three hundred years later, proved himself a great grandson of Ben in such lovely little poems as "Between Walls" and "The Red Wheelbarrow." Jonson was a classical scholar as well as a playwright and poet, and he has been called the founder of English literary criticism. So one is not surprised to find simplicity in a poem speaking against over-elaboration in a woman's costume and makeup. More than once one has seen this poem referred to as a "sonnet," but it is an unfustianed lyric assembled of two sestets made of riming couplets. In the heyday of the sonneteers, who vied to out-decorate one another with their contrived imagery, "Rare Ben Jonson" sued for divorce from "all th' adulteries of art." If you would be a rare poet, study the ninth line of this poem. Then go and check Shakespeare's "Sonnet 130."

Lady Mary Wroth (1587–1653)

My Muse Now Happy

My Muse now happy lay thy self to rest,
Sleep in the quiet of a faithful love,
Write you no more, but let these Phant'sies move
Some other hearts, wake not to new unrest.
But if you study be those thoughts addressed
To truth, which shall eternal goodness prove;
Enjoying of true joy the most, and best
The endless gain which never will remove.
Leave the discourse of Venus, and her son
To young beginners, and their brains inspire
With stories of great Love, and from that fire,
Get heat to write the fortunes they have won.
And thus leave off; what's past shows you can love,
Now let your Constancy your Honor prove.

In the early seventeenth century in England, the sonnet sequence was all the rage. Wyatt, Sydney, Drayton, Spenser, and Shakespeare were the most famous and skilled composers of these chains of love letters in rime. Sir Philip Sidney's *Astrophil and Stella* pretty well set the benchmark for the genre, and Shakespeare, of course, became the Renaissance champion with his sonnets to the "fair youth" and to the "dark lady," still mysterious personages today. Almost everyone with an education was penning sonnet sequences, the majority of which never saw print. There were lots of upperclass women writing poetry, including sonnets, a form borrowed from the Italians. Lady Mary Wroth, who was related to noblemen and poets and found lovers in that crowd, was an unorthodox woman (some say feminist) and an orthodox poet for her time. Her sonnet sequence *Pamphila to Amphilanthus* is pretty well constructed of the thoughts and feelings you might expect of someone who has kept up with the reading and writing of her circle. This sonnet closes the first section of the sequence and, in some people's opinion, the whole work. So we are not surprised to see that the poet has reached a point in her life at which she advises her muse, and thus herself, to leave off extolling the wonders of young physical love and to take up a devotion to spiritual and moral honour, as befitting poets approaching eternity. For a more complex treatment of this question, see the Keats sonnet (page 52).

Robert Herrick (1591–1674)

Delight in Disorder

A sweet disorder in the dress
Kindles in clothes a wantonness;
A lawn about the shoulders thrown
Into a fair distraction;
An erring lace which here and there
Enthralls the crimson stomacher;
A cuff neglectful, and thereby
Ribbons to flow confusedly;
A winning wave, deserving note,
In the tempestuous petticoat;
A careless shoestring, in whose tie
I see a wild civility;
Do more bewitch me than when art
Is too precise in every part.

I think that all young readers, students, poets enjoy coming across the poems of Robert Herrick, especially after working hard at the seriousness of Milton (Herrick died when *Paradise Lost* was published, by the way). In the seventeenth century it would be hard to find two less similar poems than Milton's "On the Death of a Fair Infant Dying of a Cough" and Herrick's "To the Virgins, to Make Much of Time." Herrick was one of "the sons of Ben," non-Puritan followers of Ben Jonson, so it is no surprise that Herrick's "Delight in Disorder" resembles Jonson's poem "Still to be Neat," in which less than perfection in dress and deportment is approved. Herrick was a Royalist in an age run by the Roundheads, so it is no wonder that he liked to write about and to women with appetite and humour. Yes, you see right away that we are dealing with a sonnet here, but then that it has four-beat lines, suitable for comic verse. That is a kind of disorder in itself, yes? Now listen to the end rimes. We get couplets all the way through, something more common to light verse than to Roman models, and for the first twelve lines, couplets made of imperfect rimes. You have to rime a word with a little bit of a word, or you have to reshape your mouth to rime "thrown" with the tail of "distraction." Until the final two lines — where in a regular sonnet you expect the end of an argument, here you get the poet's sudden sort of *So there!*, an orderly disordering of his established disorder.

George Herbert (1593–1633)

The Altar

A broken A L T A R, Lord, thy servant reares,
Made of a heart, and cemented with teares:
Whose parts are as thy hand did frame;
No workmans tool hath touch'd the same.
A H E A R T alone
Is such a stone,
As nothing but
Thy pow'r doth cut.
Wherefore each part
Of my hard heart
Meets in this frame,
To praise thy Name;
That, if I chance to hold my peace,
These stones to praise thee may not cease.
O let thy blessed S A C R I F I C E be mine,
And   sanctifie this A L T A R to be thine.

Like a lot of English poets in the seventeenth century, George Herbert was a clergyman. Unlike some others, he did not compose verses about erotic dalliances or fancies, instead devoting his lyrics to the church, including the actual edifice he served as rector in Wiltshire. "The Altar" is the first poem in a sequence called "The Church" from the volume *The Temple*. When I was a young student I was one of many whose attention was seized by two Herbert poems — "Easter Wings" and "The Altar," a pair of "shape" poems meant to deliver one's attention to God by way of both language and illustration. Like critics in the eighteenth century, I was a little suspicious of the mode, though I might not go as far as Addison, who called it "false wit." It was a successful way of encouraging the reader to regard the poem rather than getting it read. The first thing you notice is the shape that goes with the title. Probably the second is the uppercase lettering on a few words. Contemplation of the poem gets you to Herbert's kind of metaphysic, in which the altar becomes the poet's heart, with which he imitates Christ (who is, mysteriously, God) by sacrificing at the altar, which, remember, is the centre of the church, which is laid out as a cross, and of the act that is commemorated there. Reading the plain and asserted couplets, you are aware of Herbert's strength and his paradox, that holy speech can be uttered in the simplest of language. Golgotha was the place of sacrifice, and a holy human heart was broken there, to be joined with as in the supernatural event mentioned at the end of the poem.

Thomas Carew (1595–1640)

A Cruel Mistress

We read of kings and gods that kindly took
A pitcher fill'd with water from the brook;
But I have daily tender'd without thanks
Rivers of tears that overflow their banks.
A slaughter'd bull will appease angry Jove,
A horse the Sun, a lamb the god of love,
But she disdains the spotless sacrifice
Of a pure heart that at her altar lies.
Vesta is not displeased if her chaste urn
Do with repairèd fuel ever burn;
But my saint frowns, though to her honour'd name
I consecrate a never-dying flame.
Th' Assyrian king did none i' th' furnace throw
But those that to his image did not bow;
With bended knees I daily worship her,
Yet she consumes her own idolater.
Of such a goddess no times leave record,
That burned the temple where she was adored.

The cruel mistress, along with the coy mistress and the shy mistress, has been a subject of poetry for ages, has sometimes even been poetry herself. She continues to appear, as in the blues complaint about "Hard-hearted Hannah, the vamp of Savannah," who was seen "pouring water on a drowning man." That kind of humour, along with some raunchiness, characterizes a lot of poetry composed by the Carolinian poets of the seventeenth century and reached a climax in Carew's shocking longest poem "A Rapture." "A Cruel Mistress" is his working of the popular subject mentioned above. Here she is contrasted to the stories by Ovid and the book of Genesis in which kind hosts distinguish themselves by welcoming non-mortal beings disguised as hoboes. The unfortunate wooer of the cruel woman lists sacrifices that please the gods, thereby exaggerating his own unsatisfactory suit. The poem's comical metaphors are made of overblown images of fire and water, offering a personal little disappointment as somehow epic rejection. We will thus be prepared for the satirical anti-epics of the eighteenth century. This lover even unfavourably compares his "mistress" with Nebuchadnezzar, perhaps the Old Testament's apotheosis of cruelty. Around this time of the poem it dawns on us that while this poem might hope to cast the merciless damsel in a bad light, it has wound up portraying the hapless supplicant in a worse one.

Anne Bradstreet (1612–1672)

The Author to Her Book

Thou ill-form'd offspring of my feeble brain,
Who after birth didst by my side remain,
Till snatched from thence by friends, less wise than true,
Who thee abroad, expos'd to publick view,
Made thee in raggs, halting to th' press to trudge,
Where errors were not lessened (all may judge).
At thy return my blushing was not small,
My rambling brat (in print) should mother call,
I cast thee by as one unfit for light,
Thy Visage was so irksome in my sight;
Yet being mine own, at length affection would
Thy blemishes amend, if so I could:
I wash'd thy face, but more defects I saw,
And rubbing off a spot, still made a flaw.
I stretched thy joints to make thee even feet,
Yet still thou run'st more hobling than is meet;
In better dress to trim thee was my mind,
But nought save home-spun Cloth, i' th' house I find.
In this array 'mongst Vulgars mayst thou roam.
In Criticks hands, beware thou dost not come;
And take thy way where yet thou art not known,
If for thy Father askt, say, thou hadst none:
And for thy Mother, she alas is poor,
Which caus'd her thus to send thee out of door.

Have you ever encountered such a nice combination of humour and false modesty? Well, it is true that the manuscript of Anne Bradstreet's first book was taken "without her knowledge" to London and there published. Though she would have liked to make "corrections" to the Puritan poems of *The Tenth Muse Lately Sprung up in America,* the book was to become the first success for a woman poet of the British colonies in North America. In the U.S. they like to refer to her as "America's first published poet," though there were already numerous poets both Native and European being published from Mexico to Chile. As to her poems' being "snatched," that bit of modesty hardly fits with the last line of the poem, does it? If we think a little longer on these lines, we may come to the conclusion that we are at last being let in on the joke. We might say that we can admire Bradstreet's skill in handling poetic conventions, while enjoying her poking fun at her performance (or at us?). In later poems she would take on the question of a woman's role, poet or not, Puritan or not, and would become Britain's most western feminist writer. You did not believe, did you, that she considered her brain "feeble"? You saw that she had picked up the male poets' conventional trope of letting his offspring poem loose in the world, and then stayed with the metaphor till every foot had been trodden.

John Dryden (1631–1700)

Song: Calm Was the Even, and Clear Was the Sky

Calm was the even, and clear was the sky,
    And the new budding flowers did spring,
When all alone went Amyntas and I
    To hear the sweet nightingale sing;
I sate, and he laid him down by me;
    But scarcely his breath he could draw;
For when with a fear, he began to draw near,
    He was dash'd with A ha ha ha ha!

He blush'd to himself, and lay still for a while,
    And his modesty curb'd his desire;
But straight I convinc'd all his fear with a smile,
    Which added new flames to his fire.
O Silvia, said he, you are cruel,
    To keep your poor lover in awe;
Then once more he press'd with his hand to my breast,
    But was dash'd with A ha ha ha ha!

I knew 'twas his passion that caus'd all his fear;
    And therefore I pitied his case:
I whisper'd him softly, there's nobody near,
    And laid my cheek close to his face:
But as he grew bolder and bolder,
    A shepherd came by us and saw;
And just as our bliss we began with a kiss,
    He laugh'd out with a ha ha ha ha!

English literature teachers usually like to divide the seventeenth century between John Milton and John Dryden, with a few speaking up for John Donne. Milton prevailed during Cromwell's Puritan rule, and Dryden is generally the Restoration's man. You will go a long way trying to find humour in Milton's heavy work. He was, after all, trying to justify God's ways to Man, and the Former didn't crack many jokes, apparently. But Dryden's satirical wit continued until 1700 A.D., when he died and left the eighteenth century to the great wits Pope, Swift, Johnson and so on. "Calm was the Even" was a song in a play about sexual trickery and suspicionable love, the title being *An Evening's Love*, which should tell you something. In an age recently shaped by Puritanism and regicide, comical love stories were often disapproved of the decent folk. The wife of Samuel Pepys told him Dryden's play was indecent, and the famed diarist, who disliked Shakespeare's comedies but saw *Macbeth* nine times, attended part of *An Evening's Love* and pronounced it "smutty." His many mistresses might have snorted at him. In the play the song is sung to her would-be swain by a lass disguised as African. You can easily sing the lyrics with an unsurprising tune that leads your voice, and you may enjoy the break from tune into laughter, deciding for yourself what the latter might be taking the place of. You should know that the author was drawing upon several sporty European plays, but you can't help noticing how nicely the lines proceed as written by England's first poet laureate.

Thomas Traherne (1637–1674)

To the Same Purpose

To the same purpose: he, not long before
Brought home from nurse, going to the door
To do some little thing
He must not do within,
With wonder cries,
As in the skies
He saw the moon, "O yonder is the moon,
Newly come after me to town,
That shined at Lugwardin but yesternight,
Where I enjoyed the self-same sight."

As if it had ev'n twenty thousand faces,
It shines at once in many places;
To all the earth so wide
God doth the stars divide,
With so much art
The moon impart,
They serve us all; serve wholly every one
As if they servèd him alone.
While every single person hath such store,
'Tis want of sense that makes us poor.

Traherne manages to lose me with his first line. But a dear friend I loved and a popinjay I could not abide both professed admiration for this often-difficult poet. He is probably the most metaphysical of the metaphysical poets of the mid-seventeenth century. He was a small-town Anglican priest who lived simply, published little and thought complex thoughts that were stated in ordinary language. Maybe that is why his poetry was first discovered accidentally at the end of the nineteenth century and is still being unearthed today. "To the Same Purpose" is one of those poems that may amuse or even delight one without giving up much of its mystery. Do you remember when you were a child and didn't understand a lot of the world around you? You enjoyed those things you enjoyed and left other things to be understood when you became more experienced, and still, if there is such a thing, found God's creations sufficient to the day. Your grandfather the church minister had college degrees and a religious calling, but divinity fell on unlearned you, too. The poem is saying something not unlike your coming to the poem. Its couplets go from four beats to three, to two, and then back out to four. Maybe that matters. You go outside to visit the outhouse, and there it is, the moon, and you reflect that someone you do not even know shares its light and the rest of the sky with you and everyone else. Think of that word in the seventeenth line: "wholly."

Aphra Behn (1640–1689)

The Dream

All trembling in my arms Aminta lay,
Defending of the bliss I strove to take;
Raising my rapture by her kind delay,
Her force so charming was and weak.
The soft resistance did betray the grant,
While I pressed on the heaven of my desires;
Her rising breasts with nimbler motions pant;
Her dying eyes assume new fires.
Now to the height of languishment she grows,
And still her looks new charms put on;
Now the last mystery of Love she knows,
We sigh, and kiss: I waked, and all was done.

'Twas but a dream, yet by my heart I knew,
Which still was panting, part of it was true:
Oh how I strove the rest to have believed;
Ashamed and angry to be undeceived!

Aphra Behn showed up during the Restoration in the late seventeenth century, not as a lady of the Court trying her hand at verses, but as a woman who made her living and her mysterious reputation in all the forms of writing, most notably drama, but also poetry and fiction, including her life story. She was a leading figure in the multi-sexual literary world of post-Puritan London. Her domestic partner was a gay man and her lovers were usually Sapphic. Much of her writing opposes conventions of the time, denouncing war, the imbalance of power and freedoms between the sexes and all hegemonies political, religious and social. Thus she was a major artistic force in a changing England, while her strange name and unlikely family history were an invitation to audiences and readers who preferred fancy to realism. The first line of "The Dream" introduces the seduced Aminta, a figure borrowed from a hundred-year-old verse play by Tasso, so you see we are welcomed to a dream and exotic poetry from the beginning. Our dreamer supplies a gorgeous seduction of the virgin, all the way to "the last mystery of Love"; then in the last line before the stanza break we are jolted out of the present tense into the past, just as Aminta's conqueress is thrown from dream to reality. But please note that she is reluctant to accede, that though we are in the past, her heart holds on to the present participle — until the cruel past participle of the poem's last word.

Alexander Pope (1688–1744)

The Dying Christian to His Soul

Vital spark of heav'nly flame!
Quit, O quit this mortal frame:
Trembling, hoping, ling'ring, flying,
O the pain, the bliss of dying!
Cease, fond Nature, cease thy strife,
And let me languish into life.

Hark! they whisper; angels say,
Sister Spirit, come away!
What is this absorbs me quite?
Steals my senses, shuts my sight,
Drowns my spirits, draws my breath?
Tell me, my soul, can this be death?

The world recedes; it disappears!
Heav'n opens on my eyes! my ears
With sounds seraphic ring!
Lend, lend your wings! I mount! I fly!
O Grave! where is thy victory?
O Death! where is thy sting?

When I hear the beginning of this poem, I think of Lord Byron's "Maid of Athens, ere we part / Give, oh, give me back my heart," the beginning of a poem written one hundred years later. If you happen to read Byron, you might hear that (dis)connection between two quite opposite fellows. You might even want to visit a twentieth-century play by Brendan Behan, in which a character sings a famous airman's song written two hundred years after Pope's poem: "The Bells of Hell go ting-a-ling-a-ling, / For you but not for me. / Oh! Death, where is thy sting-a-ling-a-ling, / And Grave thy victory?", which was a parody of a popular pre-World War I song. But Pope apparently swiped a lot of his poem from a less-known poet, while claiming inspiration from the Romans. And we should not overlook the Catholic burial service lifted from Corinthians I. There's English poetry for you. Even undistinguished verse — if you listen to tea-party amateur recitations, you will hear "life" end-rimed with "strife" before the afternoon is done. Pope, known for his orderliness, finishes his first stanza with that one, then his second with "death" and "breath." We've heard that before now, too. Pope also liked an orderly paradox. No easeful death for him, but the "bliss of dying," that lets his Christian "languish into life." That, in turn, lets him climb aboard the broad back of an angel, while triumphantly lowering himself to mock the defeated grave and death's weakness. Nyah, nyah.

William Cowper (1731–1800)

Sonnet to William Wilberforce, Esq.

Thy country, Wilberforce, with just disdain,
Hears thee, by cruel men and impious, call'd
Fanatic, for thy zeal to loose th' enthrall'd
From exile, public sale, and slav'ry's chain.
Friend of the poor, the wrong'd, the fetter-gall'd,
Fear not lest labour such as thine be vain!
Thou hast achiev'd a part; hast gain'd the ear
Of Britain's senate to thy glorious cause;
Hope smiles, joy springs, and tho' cold caution pause
And weave delay, the better hour is near,
That shall remunerate thy toils severe
By peace for Afric, fenc'd with British laws.
Enjoy what thou hast won, esteem and love
From all the just on earth, and all the blest above!

A lot of ordinary poetry readers will wonder who William Wilberforce was, then spend a little time reading about progressive politics in eighteenth-century Britain. Wilberforce championed the educating of Indian colonials, the abolition of slavery and the prevention of cruelty to animals. Like the subject of his poem, Cowper was conservative and progressive, not revolutionary, though he did not share his country's enmity toward revolutionary France. He was that figure who seems to be disappearing from democracies — an upper-class banquet-goer who espoused progressive causes because his religion saw them as both logical and holy. There was a lot of that sensibility in the late eighteenth century, and Cowper was the most popular serious poet of the age. A generation later Shelley would write odes to liberty. Cowper here condenses the ode into a sonnet, and even appears to use that other public genre, the verse letter. You will notice that the poem is not presented as something private, but rather invokes the whole country's populace in its first line and Heaven's inhabitants in the last. Such poems are generally composed in unambiguous terms, even though, as here, the rime scheme might be somewhat unusual. Rereading, perhaps slowly, and certainly aloud, you will probably be impressed by lots of what schoolteachers used to call "internal rime." "Sale" rimes with "slavery," "Afric" with "fenc'd," "just" with "blest." Thus the plain becomes song, with all its curious acquirement.

Phillis Wheatley (1753–1784)

On Being Brought from Africa to America

'Twas mercy brought me from my *Pagan* land,
Taught my benighted soul to understand
That there's a God, that there's a *Saviour* too:
Once I redemption neither sought nor knew.
Some view our sable race with scornful eye,
"Their colour is a diabolic die."
Remember, *Christians*, *Negros*, black as *Cain*,
May be refin'd, and join th' angelic train.

In the eighteenth century a lot of U.S. Americans and Europeans made a fuss about Phillis Wheatley, and about Jupiter Hammon, the first Black slave in the U.S. to become a published poet. Wheatley was kidnapped in western Africa at the age of seven, carried across the Atlantic in the hold of a sailing ship and sold to a Christian man named Wheatley in Massachusetts. Hammon was born a slave earlier in the century on Long Island. He had become a poet and a slave preacher of Christianity; in fact, we have a poem by Hammon in which he welcomes the younger poet and agrees with most of her poem about her transportation. Its eleventh quatrain goes: "Thou hast left the heathen shore;/ Thro' mercy of the Lord,/ Among the heathen live no more,/ Come magnify thy God." Slaveowners with a taste for poetry and their view of Christianity liked him a lot. They were also thankful for the acquiescence of Wheatley, who had learned classical languages, modern science and European history, but they may have been discomfited by the second half of the poem we are reading. And though she was famous and provided some balm for the conscience of liberal slaveowners, she had to send to England to get her books published. After her owner died she was set "free," got married and died a scholar in penury and childbirth. She was a pioneer who made a path for later African American poets such as Frances Ellen Watkins Harper, a free woman in Baltimore who lived through the U.S. Civil War and wrote poems about the mistreatment and struggle of Black people brought to the land of the free and the home of the brave.

William Blake (1757–1827)

Ah Sun-flower!

Ah Sun-flower! weary of time,
Who countest the steps of the Sun:
Seeking after that sweet golden clime
Where the travellers journey is done.

Where the Youth pined away with desire,
And the pale Virgin shrouded in snow:
Arise from their graves and aspire.
Where my Sun-flower wishes to go.

I think that just about everyone who reads this poem for the first time falls in love with its simplicity. It is a pleasure for sure to get on with it, to walk along at the pace the second line takes. But wait! Look back at the first line. The first half expresses the admiration any of us might feel for that tall cheerful flower that likes to turn its face to the eastern sky where the source of life shines. There the poem's contradictions begin. Weary of time, the flower is totally given to it, counting the sun's steps as Sir Philip Sidney counted those of the pale moon. Maybe "ah" expresses sympathy, maybe even sadness, in addition to admiration. The contradictions continue, or maybe they are rather what Blake called "contraries." Without contraries, he wrote, there is no progression. If we were dealing with opposites, hope would be seen as the opposite of despair. People who are used to reading sonnets, in which sestets settle or generalize questions proposed in octaves, might think that Blake's first quatrain is about hope and reward and that the second quatrain introduces defeat and death. But look: after both emotions or fates are proposed, we get an image of resurrection, the snow (shroud) cast off, graves escaped, hope renewed, beyond desire's grasp. No wonder so many young readers read Blake as if he were a Buddhist. All right, progression, but here is a question I have never tried to answer: why is there a full stop after the seventh line?

William Wordsworth (1770–1850)

London, 1802

Milton! thou shouldst be living at this hour:
England hath need of thee: she is a fen
Of stagnant waters: altar, sword, and pen,
Fireside, the heroic wealth of hall and bower,
Have forfeited their ancient English dower
Of inward happiness. We are selfish men;
Oh! raise us up, return to us again;
And give us manners, virtue, freedom, power.
Thy soul was like a Star, and dwelt apart:
Thou hadst a voice whose sound was like the sea:
Pure as the naked heavens, majestic, free,
So didst thou travel on life's common way,
In cheerful godliness; and yet thy heart
The lowliest duties on herself did lay.

English poets spend a lot of their time addressing the moon and stars, you may have noticed. The moon is changeable and stars are steadfast. Traditionally, great human souls became stars and were there to be prayed to for guidance. Things must have been rotten in London at the turn of the nineteenth century. William Blake's "London," which details the sordidness of life in that city, was published eight years earlier. Its "charter'd Thames" appears here as "stagnant waters." In a note to his poem, Wordsworth wrote that it was written upon his return from a trip to post-revolutionary France. It is here that I think I see Shelley's reason for turning against his predecessor. If Wordsworth wished Milton were alive, Shelley would say that Wordsworth died before writing "The Prelude," forgetting revolution, and becoming poet laureate. In "London, 1802," Wordsworth does not contrast "stagnant" England to revolutionary France, but to the good olde days, "the heroic wealth of hall and bower." One of the adjectives he accords his hero is "majestic," certainly a quality applied to the Jehovah that Milton's Satan rebelled against. Shelley's rebels will not cuddle up to majesty, and certainly not to Blake's "Nobodaddy," but rather look to raise the forlorn above their lot. Wordsworth's view here arises from the Christlike democracy of Puritans such as Milton, but includes the conservatives' regret for "manners, virtue, freedom" that are bestowed, not taken.

Samuel Taylor Coleridge (1772–1834)

Inscription for a Fountain on a Heath

This Sycamore, oft musical with bees, —
Such tents the Patriarchs loved! O long unharmed
May all its agèd boughs o'er-canopy
The small round basin, which this jutting stone
Keeps pure from falling leaves! Long may the Spring,
Quietly as a sleeping infant's breath,
Send up cold waters to the traveller
With soft and even pulse! Nor ever cease
Yon tiny cone of sand its soundless dance,
Which at the bottom, like a fairy's page,
As merry and no taller, dances still,
Nor wrinkles the smooth surface of the fount.
Here twilight is and coolness: here is moss,
A soft seat, and a deep and ample shade.
Thou may'st toil far and find no second tree.
Drink, Pilgrim, here; here rest! and if thy heart
Be innocent, here too shalt thou refresh
Thy spirit, listening to some gentle sound,
Or passing gale or hum of murmuring bees!

What draws me back to this poem is the musical humming of the bees. How different Coleridge's inscription for this fountain from Emerson's inscription for the memorial in Concord, Massachusetts! No shots heard around the world, but "gentle sound"; no actual monument to armed patriotism, but an imagined inscription musing upon rest and refreshment for the spirit. Coleridge and Wordsworth wrote poems together in the West Country, detailing and praising the natural scene and seeing that it presented itself in symbols archaic and literary. Coleridge saw that he lived in a world of mountains, streams, plains and forests, and so did Old Testament patriarchs and Greek philosophers. As soon as we have a heath we know that we are in the English countryside. The sycamore is a high, leafy shade tree with ancestors in the ancient Mediterranean world. Coleridge's fountain is as familiar as Shelley's volcanos; it is to the earth as one's heart is to one's life — its pulse is quiet but felt, quiet as the breath of a babe. Here Coleridge sits us in imagination and offers generative silence, as Shelley would tell us "the deep truth is imageless." Yet Coleridge frames the nineteen-line poem with "musical ... murmuring" bees, even at twilight. I hear them now. What a lovely conjoining of a restful, enspiriting spot in his daily environment and a honeyed image from his usual Biblical thoughtscape! I keep coming back to this poem and looking for some word about the imagination, and it is not there, but yes, it is, isn't it?

Robert Southey (1774–1843)

Poems Concerning the Slave Trade: Sonnet 6

High in the air expos'd the slave is hung
To all the birds of Heaven, their living food!
He groans not, tho' awaked by that fierce sun
New torturers live to drink their parent blood!
He groans not, tho' the gorging vulture tear
The quivering fibre! hither gaze O ye
Who tore this man from peace and liberty!
Gaze hither ye who weigh with scrupulous care
The right and prudent; for beyond the grave
There is another world! and call to mind,
Ere your decrees proclaim to all mankind
Murder is legalized, that there the slave
Before the Eternal, "thunder-tongued shall plead
"Against the deep damnation of your deed."

When young Robert Southey was expelled from Westminster School for publicly denouncing the institution's practice of flogging, he set a pattern that the future poet laureate would trace in his poems. Like the other Romantics, he favoured social progress, but he was the most detailed and direct in his poems opposed to injustice and inequality. He championed the poor, he agitated for parliamentary reform and communal society, he spoke for women's rights and he excoriated the countries that profited in the African slave trade. The French Declaration of the Rights of Man and of the Citizen, and the U.S. Bill of Rights were issued in 1789, but eight years went by until Southey's six sonnets damning the slave trade were published. The lynching portrayed at the beginning of the sixth sonnet was available for reading 175 years before the lynching of a teenaged Black person in Alabama. The vulture that tears at the flesh of the man in Southey's poem had appeared in the first sonnet, where it was associated with "cold-hearted Commerce." That was the raptor that tore the hanged man from Africa, from his home's "peace and liberty." That last abstract noun, you will remember, was forever being announced by revolutionary France and the U.S., those two again, those along with Britain, whose "decrees proclaim to all mankind / Murder is legalized." So, all men are created equal, into *fraternité*, perhaps, but Southey suggests that "the Eternal" may have something to say about that.

Leigh Hunt (1784–1859)

Abou Ben Adhem

Abou Ben Adhem (may his tribe increase!)
Awoke one night from a deep dream of peace,
And saw — within the moonlight in his room,
Making it rich and like a lily in bloom —
An angel, writing in a book of gold.
Exceeding peace had made Ben Adhem bold,
And to the presence in the room he said,
'What writest thou?' — The vision raised its head,
And, with a look made of all sweet accord,
Answered, 'The names of those who love the Lord.'
'And is mine one?' said Abou. 'Nay, not so,'
Replied the angel. Abou spoke more low,
But cheerly still, and said, 'I pray thee, then,
Write me as one that loves his fellow men.'

The angel wrote and vanished. The next night
It came again with a great wakening light,
And showed the names whom love of God had blessed,
And lo! Ben Adhem's name led all the rest.

When we were kids, various Christian kids by category, it was pretty well agreed among our parents, or at least the sober ones, that the purpose of poetry was pretty well the purpose of sermons, to give us examples of good deeds and decent behaviour or to warn against their opposites. To teach and guide, and to adhere to a proper rime scheme. That's what the riming couplet was for, especially the one at the end of a sonnet. *What is the message of the poem?* teachers and students would enquire of one another, and according to what I have seen on the internet, they are still urged to do so. As my childhood seeped away I eventually wondered where that notion of a "message" came from. But from early childhood my companions and I were surrounded by such propositions. Aesop's fables and those of Uncle Remus always had a lesson to teach via narrative. The church minister had a subject to put out there every week: he would read a relevant passage from the Bible and then tell a parallel modern story. We are all a little like Joseph's brethren, aren't we? A popular magazine had a feature in which we are told something like, "Here is a watchbird watching a fibber. Here is a watchbird watching you. Have you been a fibber today?" Leigh Hunt, like most of the Romantic poets and novelists, was an Orientalist. He followed a common pattern when he went to the mysterious East to set us on exotic ground, then set about showing that the foreign is not so strange after all. In "Abou Ben Adhem," he first introduces that eventual Sufi saint (then imitates a Muslim aside), before proving that God is consistent among religions. But on the way, he baffles me: if you were to awaken to see a shining angel sitting in your room and writing in a golden book, would your first question be a calm and friendly, "What are you writing there"?

George Gordon, Lord Byron (1788–1824)

To Eliza

Eliza, what fools are the Mussulman sect,
Who to woman deny the soul's future existence!
Could they see thee, Eliza, they'd own their defect,
And this doctrine would meet with a general resistance.

Had their prophet possess'd half an atom of sense,
He ne'er would have woman from paradise driven;
Instead of his houris, a flimsy pretence,
With woman alone he had peopled his heaven.

Yet still, to increase your calamities more,
Not content with depriving your bodies of spirit,
He allots one poor husband to share amongst four! –
With souls you'd dispense; but this last, who could bear it?

His religion to please neither party is made;
On husbands 'tis hard, to the wives most uncivil;
Still I can't contradict, what so oft has been said,
'Though women are angels, yet wedlock's the devil.'

Does Byron make you uncomfortable yet? Good! There are four things we know about Lord Byron, all of which have some bearing on this poem, which comprised ten quatrains when it was first published in 1806, the last six being an argument against wedlock.

1. He was the most famous of the English Romantic poets in his time.
2. His poems are a little amateurish when compared with those of Wordsworth, Coleridge, Keats, Shelley, etc. So, his life (swimming the Hellespont, etc.) is more exciting than his poetry.
3. He had, as they say, countless sexual affairs, sometimes leaving the resultant children to be cared for by others, including Shelley.
4. He became a hero in Greece for his efforts to help free the Greeks from the rule of the Ottoman Empire. His name is now all over Greece, including the package of a popular cigarette.

In the first four lines of this poem, we see the way he could conjoin politics and courtliness, while doggedly walking his quasi-anapests. (Byron, like many satirical poets, liked anapests — see his poem "The Destruction of Sennacherib.") For a long time I let myself be puzzled by the logic of the first quatrain of "To Eliza." If the Muslims could but see Elizabeth Pigot, the poet's neighbour and friend from youth, they would amend the Quran and allow women to have immortal souls. Nowadays I just give up logic and say okay to poetic miracles. The last six quatrains follow the seeming feminism of the first four with references to the Christian Bible.

Percy Bysshe Shelley (1792–1822)

Mutability

We are as clouds that veil the midnight moon;
　　How restlessly they speed, and gleam, and quiver,
Streaking the darkness radiantly! — yet soon
　　Night closes round, and they are lost forever.

Or like forgotten lyres, whose dissonant strings
　　Give various response to each varying blast,
To whose frail frame no second motion brings
　　One mood or modulation like the last.

We rest. — A dream has power to poison sleep;
　　We rise. — One wandering thought pollutes the day;
We feel, conceive or reason, laugh or weep;
　　Embrace fond woe, or cast our cares away:

It is the same! — For, be it joy or sorrow,
　　The path of its departure still is free:
Man's yesterday may ne'er be like his morrow;
　　Nought may endure but mutability!

If you spent your childhood in orchard country, you early perceived the double nature of time. You saw the cherries arrive on branches where blossoms had been doing their doing several weeks earlier. Yet you had seen this happen before and were likely to say that the cherries were back in the trees. So the child begins to know that time is difficult to distinguish from space. He was also learning that writing and reading were not all that different from one another. He would read a lot of poetry and see that poets have always been interested in change, and its opposite that doesn't exist. Poets have always been interested in difference, which they sometimes portray in similies. Poets are interested in change and the paradoxes it presents. In a poem called "The Kingfishers," Charles Olson said, "What does not change/ is the will to change." So young Shelley, in one of his easiest poems. He joins other Romantic poets in choosing the Aeolian lyre (sometimes called the Aeolian harp) as his metaphor for poetic utterance. Aeolus was the ancient Greek keeper of the winds, and the Aeolian lyre was placed in a tree to be played, as the trees are, by the wind, perhaps the most often-used image for the relationship between nature and art. In "Ode to the West Wind," Shelley asks that the wind make him its lyre as the forest itself is. In "Mutability," things seem to be proceeding as they should, in a poem of four stable stanzas, each composed of four stable lines with regulated end rime and metered iambic. Yet the third stanza, full of verbs, reminds us not to expect stasis but the endurance of its alleged opposite.

John Keats (1795–1821)

Bright Star, Would I Were Stedfast as Thou Art

Bright star, would I were stedfast as thou art —
    Not in lone splendour hung aloft the night
And watching, with eternal lids apart,
    Like nature's patient, sleepless Eremite,
The moving waters at their priestlike task
    Of pure ablution round earth's human shores,
Or gazing on the new soft-fallen mask
    Of snow upon the mountains and the moors —
No — yet still stedfast, still unchangeable,
    Pillow'd upon my fair love's ripening breast,
To feel for ever its soft fall and swell,
    Awake for ever in a sweet unrest,
Still, still to hear her tender-taken breath,
And so live ever — or else swoon to death.

Sonnets are usually about resolution, often proposing a question or conflict in their beginning and answering or generalizing it in their conclusion. John Keats fools with the system in this sonnet, opening with a wish for perfection beyond human reach and finishing with a couplet, riming "breath" with "death," the mortal human summing up. A couplet at the end of a Shakespearean sonnet or a Shakespearean scene signifies that something — an argument or an important bit of plot — has been settled. Keats loved, or at least greatly liked, paradox. All he knew about living was dying, unfortunate man. In this poem he first envies the steadfastness of the "lone" star, while using a first present participle about its observing of Earth's ever-"moving" waters — our most often-employed symbol of (paradox alert) constant change. Keats's sestet, like his octave, is made of one sentence, and though it begins with adjectives that mean steady, it will offer a third present participle in describing a human breast in contrast to the distant star. Keats's speaker would feel it "forever," but it would be in never-stopping loveable motion. The star's eye will never close, but Keats would choose a wonderful alert drowse, his happy head lying (and here follows one of the most marvellous lines in English poetry) "Awake for ever in a sweet unrest," that last word falling between and softly insisting on the meaningful rime of "breast" and "breath." The poet doesn't really want to be steadfast; he wants to ease into eternity without getting there. His is an ethereal version of the male sexual paradox described by poet Robert Kroetsch in his essay "For Play and Entrance."

Ralph Waldo Emerson (1803–1882)

Concord Hymn

By the rude bridge that arched the flood,
   Their flag to April's breeze unfurled,
Here once the embattled farmers stood
   And fired the shot heard 'round the world.

The foe long since in silence slept;
   Alike the conqueror silent sleeps;
And Time the ruined bridge has swept
   Down the dark stream which seaward creeps.

On this green bank, by this soft stream,
   We set today a votive stone;
That memory may their deed redeem,
   When, like our sires, our sons are gone.

Spirit, that made those heroes dare
   To die, and leave their children free,
Bid Time and Nature gently spare
   The shaft we raise to them and thee.

Sung at the Completion of the Battle Monument, July 4, 1837

A hymn, since ancient times, is a kind of song in praise of some god, such as Apollo, or some semi-immortal hero. Concord is the town near Boston where the great armed American treason or revolution (depending on your point of view) began. Emerson, a straight-ahead U.S. patriot, makes no note of the irony in the town's name. The shots heard around the bridge were fired in 1775. Emerson's poem was perhaps not sung but spoken when a commemorative obelisk was erected in 1837, and first published in 1847. Emerson is still a much-loved U.S. essayist and is often referred to as a philosopher, very useful in university undergraduate courses. As a poet, he was in a way the Robert Frost of his time, often quoted, often met with the words "how true" or "well said." Sometimes he did smudge the grammar in a poem — see the verb tense in line five here. It would not be the last time our language was wounded by the outbreak of war. Today, there are numberless monuments to dead soldiers all over the U.S., whose lethal patriotism has been continuous for two and a half centuries. Perhaps I am too harsh on Emerson. A lot of people who normally think well of humankind become reverential around the soil of the war dead. Here we might find a simple irony in that there is concord among them, both armies sleeping while Time proves itself longer than enmity. Still, I prefer the Spirit that Shelley addressed to this one that made "heroes" dead.

Elizabeth Barrett Browning (1806–1861)

XLIV [from *Sonnets from the Portuguese*]

Beloved, thou hast brought me many flowers
Plucked in the garden, all the summer through,
And winter, and it seemed as if they grew
In this close room, nor missed the sun and showers.
So, in the like name of that love of ours,
Take back these thoughts which here unfolded too,
And which on warm and cold days I withdrew
From my heart's ground. Indeed, those beds and bowers
Be overgrown with bitter weeds and rue,
And wait thy weeding; yet here's eglantine,
Here's ivy! — take them, as I used to do
Thy flowers, and keep them where they shall not pine.
Instruct thine eyes to keep their colours true,
And tell thy soul, their roots are left in mine.

When I was a youngster, Elizabeth Barrett Browning was generally included among the important poets you should read, along with her husband and others such as the guy who wrote "Elegy Written in a Country Churchyard." We recited lines from her best-known sonnets, then later satirized them. Nowadays I never hear her lines spoken. And why Portuguese? No, these are not translations, but rather a reference to the pet name by which Robert Browning addressed his wife. One of her sonnets even mentioned it (without revealing it). You will notice that the poems, published in 1850, continue the conventions of the sonnet sequence, in which the poet or her speaker tells all the angles of her adoration for the loved one. Browning told her that hers was the best such sequence since Shakespeare's, and there was a time when lots of high school teachers agreed with him. One thing that I do admire about this poem is the way the poet begins with plain clear traditional rime and iambic meter, suggesting that the poem will be easy to follow, then proceeds to tangle a conceit that begins by equalizing flowers and poems and identifying her heart with the nutritive soil of their garden. Not satisfied with that complex metaphor, she introduces sadness, sensed in the necessary "bitter weeds and rue". Here's the kind of strange loop we could all go off on. Rue is a smelly herb native to the Balkan Peninsula, and the original name of Browning's sequence was "Sonnets from the Bosnian."

Henry Wadsworth Longfellow (1807–1882)

The Arrow and the Song

I shot an arrow into the air,
It fell to earth, I knew not where;
For, so swiftly it flew, the sight
Could not follow it in its flight.

I breathed a song into the air,
It fell to earth, I knew not where;
For who has sight so keen and strong,
That it can follow the flight of song?

Long, long afterward, in an oak
I found the arrow, still unbroke;
And the song, from beginning to end,
I found again in the heart of a friend.

Most of a century ago, when my mother was a schoolgirl, Mr. Longfellow was still considered a serious and accomplished poet. He sold us Hiawatha and Evangeline and the midnight ride of Paul Revere, after all. He was growing up while Wordsworth was being groomed as poet laureate, and he soon set about making himself the most popular poet in the U.S.A. This would mean combining patriotism and easily consumable narratives and verse forms. He let it be known that his family came over on the *Mayflower*, and for most of his life he lived in George Washington's old wartime headquarters. It worked, as he became the first U.S. poet to make a fortune by his verses. Most literate U.S. Americans know the first two lines of "The Arrow and the Song." When I first heard the poem I thought it was pretty neat, but I had some questions. Isn't it pretty reckless to shoot an arrow into the air? How can you say that it fell to earth if it was to be found long afterward (if this repeated word comes soon after "follow," could he have been playing with his own name?) in a tree? Isn't the third line of the first stanza misleading, and was the coming rime worth the confusion? Would it not be hearing rather than sight that would attempt, unsuccessfully perhaps, to follow the song that was to fall to earth? Isn't it kind of amateurish or ungrammatical to say "unbroke" instead of "unbroken"? Wouldn't the latter improve the poem, you know, *breaking* the tedium? The penultimate line — is its hobbling supposed to prepare us for the extra steps of the last line? Well, I guess this poem is a nice lesson in mythmaking or at least metaphor. I mean, it's good for Longfellow's reputation that it was not an arrow found in the heart of a friend.

Edgar Allan Poe (1809–1849)

Sonnet — To Science

Science! true daughter of Old Time thou art!
   Who alterest all things with thy peering eyes.
Why preyest thou thus upon the poet's heart,
   Vulture, whose wings are dull realities?
How should he love thee? or how deem thee wise,
   Who wouldst not leave him in his wandering
To seek for treasure in the jewelled skies,
   Albeit he soared with an undaunted wing?
Hast thou not dragged Diana from her car,
   And driven the Hamadryad from the wood
To seek a shelter in some happier star?
   Hast thou not torn the Naiad from her flood,
The Elfin from the green grass, and from me
The summer dream beneath the tamarind tree?

For hundreds of years, wherever writers have written their stories of human behaviour, there has been a difference between realism and mystery. In the nineteenth century the difference became increasingly one between science and fancy. Edgar Allan Poe had a great following in France, and it persists today. Emile Zola, though, wrote that as the scientific method had transformed the practice of medicine in his country, so it should be encouraged to guide the writing of fiction. His work, dubbed naturalism, had a strong influence on subsequent fiction in Britain and the United States. Poe's sonnet might have seen it coming. It starts with a satirical nod to science before calling it a bird of prey, and a nasty one at that. Its wings of dull reality are set against the poet's wings that could take him fearlessly to the stars. Lovely figures of ancient myth have been attacked by this vulture — Diana, goddess of the moon, hamadryads (whose expulsion will mean the destruction of the forest itself), naiads (who are the spirits necessary to streams and lakes and thus life itself), and the elfin of the grass. It is as if Poe were given an eye that could see what we with our weapons have done to our planet's living body. A lot of people think of Poe as the author of horror stories and fanciful verse. They ought to read this sonnet aloud, its rhythm and sounds so moving, the near perfection of its last three lines. Sonnets were invented as love poems; Poe the critic never forgets that.

Alfred, Lord Tennyson (1809–1892)

The Miller's Daughter

It is the miller's daughter,
And she is grown so dear, so dear,
That I would be the jewel
That trembles at her ear:
For hid in ringlets day and night,
I'd touch her neck so warm and white.

And I would be the girdle
About her dainty, dainty waist,
And her heart would beat against me,
In sorrow and in rest:
And I should know if it beat right,
I'd clasp it round so close and tight.

And I would be the necklace,
And all day long to fall and rise
Upon her balmy bosom,
With her laughter or her sighs:
And I would lie so light, so light,
I scarce should be unclasped at night.

I have never read much Tennyson, and I would wager that he doesn't have a wide readership in the twenty-first century. But he was the most famous and respected of the Victorian poets of England and its worldwide empire. He produced poems that schoolchildren had to learn by heart, such as "The Charge of the Light Brigade." He wrote a sentimental long poem entitled "The Miller's Daughter," and tossed off this easy, slightly naughty eighteen-liner with the same name. It is a tribute to the poet's skill that he could compose a tuneful item with such gracefulness on such an oft-used frame, and that he could make a pretty verse out of what had long been the subject of ribald humour. In the verses' progress from the country girl's ear to her neck, torso, finally bosom, the poem proceeds with sweetness, and at the same time with softly deft lasciviousness. I like the aspirant's choice of objects he would change places with — a jewel, then a girdle (not underwear but a belt or sash, such as is worn by Tennyson's Lady of Shalott, her symbol of both innocence and magical power), and finally more jewels, a necklace to lie upon her bosom, more particularly, between her breasts. If you like some pepper in your poetry, you may check the pronunciation at the end of line four. If you seem to notice an unnamable erotic music running through the poem, try playing with gender reversals and the like. "Her laughter and her sighs" — not a bad response from the readers, too.

Robert Browning (1812–1889)

Home-Thoughts, from Abroad

Oh, to be in England
Now that April's there,
And whoever wakes in England
Sees, some morning, unaware,
That the lowest boughs and the brushwood sheaf
Round the elm-tree bole are in tiny leaf,
While the chaffinch sings on the orchard bough
In England – now!

And after April, when May follows,
And the whitethroat builds, and all the swallows!
Hark, where my blossomed pear-tree in the hedge
Leans to the field and scatters on the clover
Blossoms and dewdrops – at the bent spray's edge –
That's the wise thrush; he sings each song twice over,
Lest you should think he never could recapture
The first fine careless rapture!
And though the fields look rough with hoary dew,
All will be gay when noontide wakes anew
The buttercups, the little children's dower
– Far brighter than this gaudy melon-flower!

You will hear Robert Browning at his best if you speak, or nearly sing, the first stanza aloud, so that the sound is prominent and the words seem to serve music rather than some metronome. The metronome asserts itself in the second stanza, and it is no fluke that the first line brings no news other than the calendar we learned as children. Maybe it is because of that unexciting information that the poet has to spike his twenty lines with four exclamation marks! Still, we are impressed with the way Browning *speaks*, with very little in the way of the unnatural structures we have noticed in many earlier poets who had to hold tight to the reins of both rime scheme and sentences. He was writing thus midway through the nineteenth century, during which the English poets hung out in southern Europe, while England was being treated to relentless winter rains. He was following Coleridge, Southey, Byron, Keats and Shelley, who could one way or another afford time in the Mediterranean after the disposal of Napoleon made it possible to get there again. Famous for his obscurity and love of the unfamiliar, as seen in *Sordello*, his long poem about a thirteenth-century troubadour poet encountered in Dante's great epic, he would interest Ezra Pound, who began *his* epic by addressing Browning and *his* Sordello instead of the usual invoking of a muse. But in his "Home-Thoughts," Browning opts for the plain simple (sentimental) beauty of English buttercups over exotic garden blooms.

Emily Brontë (1818–1848)

All Hushed and Still

All hushed and still within the house;
Without — all wind and driving rain;
But something whispers to my mind,
Through rain and through the wailing wind,
Never again.
Never again? Why not again?
Memory has power as real as thine.

Emily Brontë, according to some readers, wrote the most admirable English novel of the nineteenth century. She was born a year after Jane Austen died. There was a fold in consciousness then: Austen wrote orderly books about women striving for orderly lives; Brontë lived where ghostly fingers scraped at windows. Emily Dickinson, born during Brontë's short lifetime, understood what it was to live inside a house surrounded by uncertainty. After Dickinson died, a Brontë poem was the only one read at her funeral. Reading the one we have here is a pretty good preparation for reading Dickinson's poems; it seems a little like reading notes for a poem, shorthand inside a creative head. Yet it begins with the dumdedum iambic boots of so many Dickinson poems. If you approach poems with a literal mind, as I do, you hear the verb in "hushed" and wonder what caused it to happen. You are not long tempted to read "still" as "yet," but you sense that "within" is used rather than "in" for more than the iamb. Why is it suddenly quiet inside, what is happening outside, you wonder, and Brontë knew you would, and next takes you there. It's an awful Yorkshire storm, too furious for a complete sentence. While adjectives took care of inside, nouns attack from outside. However, Brontë leads you even further inside, where "something" whispers louder than the wind, "Never again." And that's the main thing in the poem, and why the poem is good — there are at least two questions more important than the two denoted by question marks.

Walt Whitman (1819–1892)

I Hear America Singing

I hear America singing, the varied carols I hear,
Those of mechanics, each one singing his as it should be
blithe and strong,
The carpenter singing his as he measures his plank or beam,
The mason singing his as he makes ready for work, or leaves
off work,
The boatman singing what belongs to him in his boat, the
deckhand singing on the steamboat deck,
The shoemaker singing as he sits on his bench, the hatter
singing as he stands,
The wood-cutter's song, the ploughboy's on his way in the
morning, or at noon intermission or at sundown,
The delicious singing of the mother, or of the young wife at
work, or of the girl sewing or washing,
Each singing what belongs to him or her and to none else,
The day what belongs to the day — at night the party of
young fellows, robust, friendly,
Singing with open mouths their strong melodious songs.

At first you might wonder whether Whitman means that he is hearing workers in the United States or workers in all of America from Tierra del Fuego to Baffin Island. I think it's possible that he means both — the nineteenth-century Whitman followed the eighteenth-century Thomas Jefferson in looking forward to a time when his country will have gobbled up the whole hemisphere. Such gobbling was called Manifest Destiny by some, *Lebensraum* by some others. Whitman's notion of song accompanying work is pretty common. Whistle while you work, sang Jiminy Cricket, remember? He was a fictional character in the movies, as were all those melodious slaves "singing on the steamboat deck," and in the hot cotton fields, and among the stones they piled to build the White House. The slaves who had a lot to do with building Whitman's country did not own anything, not even themselves, and so were not referred to in the ninth line, "Each singing what belongs to him or her and to none else." Whitman the patriot liked the idea of a country made of individual states, a nation made of individual workers, and so on. His favourite poetic form was the list, as found in the Bible, a volume made up of individual books. The Ten Commandments, the begats, the Sermon on the Mount are some influential lists. Whitman in his poem lists various individuals singing, to be echoed, you might say, in his famous poem "Song of Myself." You may sometime hear someone reading "I Hear America Singing," but I wonder whether you have tried singing it.

Matthew Arnold (1822–1888)

Youth and Calm

'Tis death! and peace, indeed, is here,
And ease from shame, and rest from fear.
There's nothing can dismarble now
The smoothness of that limpid brow.
But is a calm like this, in truth,
The crowning end of life and youth,
And when this boon rewards the dead,
Are all debts paid, has all been said?
And is the heart of youth so light,
Its step so firm, its eye so bright,
Because on its hot brow there blows
A wind of promise and repose
From the far grave, to which it goes;
Because it hath the hope to come,
One day, to harbour in the tomb?
Ah no, the bliss youth dreams is one
For daylight, for the cheerful sun,
For feeling nerves and living breath —
Youth dreams a bliss on this side death.
It dreams a rest, if not more deep,
More grateful than this marble sleep;
It hears a voice within it tell:
Calm's not life's crown, though calm is well.
'Tis all perhaps which man acquires,
But 'tis not what our youth desires.

I think that it may be interesting that Arnold published this poem halfway through his adult life, and that it appeared in *Early Poems*. He would become the third great Victorian poet, they say, the one whose major calling was criticism and whose reputation was built upon sensible argument. You can't help noticing here that his rhythm is rational iambic tetrameter and that his end rime is made of couplets, the favourite discursive method of the eighteenth-century poets, whose aim was often satirical criticism or reasoned explanation. You can tell that Arnold wants to argue, because after the opening four lines have made their case, he offers a rhetorical question starting with the word "But." And you can almost hear a book being slapped shut in one hand as soon as the final couplet has been pronounced. The middle-aged poet already knows that a human life is a tragedy toward its conclusion, but it has not been all that long since his own youth. There is a kind of pleasure in reading poems such as this one, with the invitation to murmur "how true, how sad but how true." If you can get past wondering why the poem opens with that short exclamation and what the reference might be, you can find yourself being pleased by Arnold's weaving of tonal music through rime that does not wait for the right margin to occur — peace and ease, brow and crown, dead and debts, bliss and bliss, dismarble and marble — *etc.*

Frances Ellen Watkins Harper (1825–1911)

The Slave Auction

The sale began — young girls were there,
    Defenseless in their wretchedness,
Whose stifled sobs of deep despair
    Revealed their anguish and distress.

And mothers stood, with streaming eyes,
    And saw their dearest children sold;
Unheeded rose their bitter cries,
    While tyrants bartered them for gold.

And woman, with her love and truth —
    For these in sable forms may dwell —
Gazed on the husband of her youth,
    With anguish none may paint or tell.

And men, whose sole crime was their hue,
    The impress of their Maker's hand,
And frail and shrinking children too,
    Were gathered in that mournful band.

Ye who have laid your loved to rest,
    And wept above their lifeless clay,
Know not the anguish of that breast,
    Whose loved are rudely torn away.

Ye may not know how desolate
    Are bosoms rudely forced to part,
And how a dull and heavy weight
    Will press the life-drops from the heart.

You will see that we have come quite a way from Phillis Wheatley's grateful poem about being brought from Africa to America. Frances Harper was an African American born in 1825 to free parents in the slave state of Maryland, and twenty-one years later she published her first book of poems. As well as writing, she gave her life to emancipation, women's suffrage and efforts to persuade the U.S. government to participate in progressive reform. She helped escaped slaves to get to Canada and worked as a teacher, journalist, orator and social worker. Born a year after Lord Byron died during his efforts to gain freedom for the Greek people from Turkish tyranny, she spent her long life working toward freedom from American tyranny. She was not shy about such words — see line seven in "The Slave Auction." Her career as poet, novelist and speechwriter preceded the U.S. Civil War and followed it as she travelled the postwar south, working for impoverished women. White politicians told her to go back where she came from. "The Slave Auction" is a poem made of calm iambs and expert quatrains about the heart-tearing life experienced by her own forebears and others who were created human by God and handled in America as livestock. To hear the rhythms of William Blake's "every infant's cry of fear" applied to the American scene by a woman of colour in the land wrenched from British hands by slavers gives reason for anguish and for hope.

Christina Rossetti (1830–1894)

After Death

The curtains were half drawn, the floor was swept
And strewn with rushes, rosemary and may
Lay thick upon the bed on which I lay,
Where through the lattice ivy-shadows crept.
He leaned above me, thinking that I slept
And could not hear him; but I heard him say,
'Poor child, poor child': and as he turned away
Came a deep silence, and I knew he wept.
He did not touch the shroud, or raise the fold
That hid my face, or take my hand in his,
Or ruffle the smooth pillows for my head:
He did not love me living; but once dead
He pitied me; and very sweet it is
To know he still is warm though I am cold.

Halfway through the nineteenth century in England, Elizabeth Barrett Browning and Christina Rossetti were considered, even by famous male poets, the two premier women poets in the language. If you are like me, you don't know their work all that well. You do know that Rossetti was an important figure among the Pre-Raphaelites, so you expect poetry about death and its decorative mystery. But are you prepared for a poem spoken not by the grieving man but by the pitied maiden able to make a sonnet though no longer among the living? Such a feat, perhaps, deserves forgiveness for the misplaced modifier at the end of the twelfth line. Given the magic and the unrealistic situation, we should likely expect weighty symbolism, asking ourselves or an expert what might be symbolized by "rosemary and may" lying on a death bed. We do remember stressed Ophelia's saying, "There's rosemary, that's for remembrance," and that Pre-Raphaelite John Everett Millais made a famous painting of Ophelia floating down a stream surrounded by flowers. But the mayflower (lily of the valley) is associated with spring and rebirth. Perhaps while she was festooning her scene with mayflowers Rossetti was thinking of life after death, though except in the title, that concept is not obvious here. The whole scene is described in the past tense. The speaker, in order to speak the poem, must still be around, remembering, and decorating the poem as someone has decorated and swept the room. As things have gone in these later years, I have heard Rossetti called a feminist, but I don't get that sense from the morbid self-sacrifice in the poem's sestet.

Emily Dickinson (1830–1886)

I'm Nobody! Who Are You?

I'm Nobody! Who are you?
Are you — Nobody — too?
Then there's a pair of us!
Don't tell! they'd advertise — you know!

How dreary — to be — Somebody!
How public — like a Frog —
To tell one's name — the livelong June —
To an admiring Bog!

Very few of Emily Dickinson's 1800 poems were in print before she died. As you can see, she devised her own system of punctuation, and she knew that punctuation is equal to members of the alphabet when it comes to instructions on sounds and their changes. Unfortunately, when her family found all her packets of handwritten poems, they and others said, *Oh, poor little Emily; let's correct these things, let's get rid of those capital letters and dashes. Let's improve those rimes.* Fortunately, an intelligent man named Thomas H. Johnson edited a complete edition of Dickinson's poems in 1955, with the author still in them. It is only somewhat unfortunate that all the dashes had to be equal in length. As with almost all poems, you should be reading Dickinson's lines aloud. Take the fifth line, for example. Pause for half a second after "dreary" and maybe a bit longer after "to be." Hear what happens when you say, "How dreary to be somebody," instead. Yet that is what editors and publishers wanted us to say for sixty-five years. You will notice that because of the pause and the capital letter (and the exclamation point) you said "Somebody" with more attention than you might have. This is the way you read an Emily Dickinson poem. Most of them, written but not shared, have no title, so you have to wonder: who is *you?* Is *you* the reader? A silent ghost in the room? A convention unlike the ones her early editors wanted her to observe? Despite this question, the argument of this poem is not difficult to parse, even for a Nobody.

Thomas Hardy (1840–1928)

The Darkling Thrush

I leant upon a coppice gate
    When Frost was spectre-grey,
And Winter's dregs made desolate
    The weakening eye of day.
The tangled bine-stems scored the sky
    Like strings of broken lyres,
And all mankind that haunted nigh
    Had sought their household fires.

The land's sharp features seemed to be
    The Century's corpse outleant,
His crypt the cloudy canopy,
    The wind his death-lament.
The ancient pulse of germ and birth
    Was shrunken hard and dry,
And every spirit upon earth
    Seemed fervourless as I.

At once a voice arose among
    The bleak twigs overhead
In a full-hearted evensong
    Of joy illimited;
An aged thrush, frail, gaunt, and small,
    In blast-beruffled plume,
Had chosen thus to fling his soul
    Upon the growing gloom.

So little cause for carolings
   Of such ecstatic sound
Was written on terrestrial things
   Afar or nigh around,
That I could think there trembled through
   His happy good-night air
Some blessed Hope, whereof he knew
   And I was unaware.

In his bleak new century's eve poem, the great novelist
Thomas Hardy batters two of the favourite symbols used by
the English Romantic poets — the news-bringing bird and
the Aeolian lyre. The Romantics had been, for the most part,
voices of revolution and champions of nature. But on the eve
of the twentieth century, Hardy was aware of no blithe spirit
such as Shelley's skylark or Keats's nightingale. His blast-
beruffled little bird barely lived under a sky scored by a forlorn natural lyre that was tangled and broken. The wind is
no breeze and plays no sweet song on that instrument, only
a death lament. So much for nature. You can imagine how
many people were writing poems for the new century, the
traditional anthems and hymns filled with conventional hope.
But Hardy, whose great uncheerful novels are behind him and
whose great uncheerful poems are yet to come, lets us know
in poetry's numerous ways that the man who "leant" on a gate
to nature would appear to be leaning where the old century's
corpse "outleant." Then, from a gigantic grave of nature, this
scruffy little old bird throws out its soul in song, traditionally
urging any nearby poet to do likewise. All right, says the old
novelist, whose recent books have garnered hostility from
readers and fellow writers, you may know some good news, but
you cannot prove it by me. Go find your Noah somewhere else.

Gerard Manley Hopkins (1844–1889)

The Windhover   *To Christ our Lord*

I caught this morning morning's minion, king-
   dom of daylight's dauphin, dapple-dawn-drawn Falcon,
     in his riding
Of the rolling level underneath him steady air, and striding
High there, how he rung upon the rein of a wimpling wing
In his ecstasy! then off, off forth on swing,
   As a skate's heel sweeps smooth on a bow-bend: the hurl
     and gliding
Rebuffed the big wind. My heart in hiding
Stirred for a bird, – the achieve of, the mastery of the thing!

Brute beauty and valour and act, oh, air, pride, plume, here
   Buckle! AND the fire that breaks from thee then, a billion
Times told lovelier, more dangerous, O my chevalier!

No wonder of it: shéer plód makes plough down sillion
Shine, and blue-bleak embers, ah my dear,
   Fall, gall themselves, and gash gold-vermillion.

When my friends and I were undergraduate poetry readers and would-be writers, we spent a lot of time re-reading and reciting this sonnet. I don't think there is any poem I have read as often as this one, certainly none I have spoken aloud as often. You can find out that Hopkins was raised in an artistic high Anglican family, then became a Jesuit priest. He destroyed his poems and drawings, determined to refuse vainglory and serve his God and His people with humility. Thank God or one of His interpreters, Hopkins went on to write beautiful poems and genius poetics, but he did not choose to see them published. The argument for publication can be stated simply: worldly beauty should be portrayed not as a distraction from the Divine but as a metaphor for God's greater gift that humans may not yet see. Shelley posed a somewhat similar idea, but replaced the Christian God with the transcendental imagination. Anyway, we students saw and heard that "shéer plód" directs us to take off our iambic pants and read the poem aloud. Time later for looking up what *sillion* means. With the glorious sound in one's ears, one can attend the images. Given time, you could write a whole book about this poem. Looking at a small raptor, Hopkins tells us that in diving to earth the kestrel appears a billion times more beautiful than it did riding the clouds, as Christ the lord and redeemer proved himself in his non-gnostic descent into total sacrifice.

Alice Brown (1857–1948)

Cloistered

Seal thou the window! Yea, shut out the light
And bar my door to all the airs of spring.
Yet in my cell, concealed from curious sight,
Here will I sit and sing.
Deaf, blind, and wilt Thou have me dumb, also,
Telling in silence these sad beads of days?
So let it be: though no sweet numbers flow,
My breath shall be Thy praise.

Yea, though Thou slay the life wherein men see
The upward-mounting flame, the failing spark,
My heart of love, that heart Thou gavest me,
Shall beat on in the dark.

In reading a lot of poems by famous poets recently, I noticed that our most hallowed makers left behind a lot of amateurish little verses. Though she was famous for many years, she isn't anymore, and I had no memory of having encountered Alice Brown's work before starting on my project; but I must say that her poem "Cloistered" is at least as good as some of the rimes left us (sometimes against their wishes, to be sure) by your Byrons or your Popes. How sweet it is to my ear to hear her attacking the iamb every time it threatens to walk over us. I can hear her critics accusing her of a failure to sustain the time-honoured meter. It is true that Alice Brown was a life-strife poet, but she bequeathed us at least one pretty good poem, and it deserves to live longer than all her biannual fiction volumes. For one thing, it is not doggedly spelled out; there is a little mystery, or at least puzzlement. The first two lines of the third stanza are not immediately consumable. The first line of the first stanza announces that the iambs will not lull us. The first line of the second stanza makes for a fetching break in the grammar, bringing the speaker closer to the reader. That line seems to be addressed to God the creator, and spoken by an unsubdued daughter. She's as "undisciplined" as any Donne. She lets us know that you don't have to pitch in unneeded words just to finish a sonnet. Read the poem over and again. That daughter has spunk and tells her creator it's his responsibility, her faith.

Archibald Lampman (1861–1899)

We Too Shall Sleep

Not, not for thee,
Belovèd child, the burning grasp of life
Shall bruise the tender soul. The noise, and strife,
And clamor of midday thou shalt not see;
But wrapped for ever in thy quiet grave,
Too little to have known the earthly lot,
Time's clashing hosts above thine innocent head,
Wave upon wave,
Shall break, or pass as with an army's tread,
And harm thee not.

A few short years
We of the living flesh and restless brain
Shall plumb the deeps of life and know the strain,
The fleeting gleams of joy, the fruitless tears;
And then at last when all is touched and tried,
Our own immutable night shall fall, and deep
In the same silent plot, O little friend,
Side by thy side,
In peace that changeth not, nor knoweth end,
We too shall sleep.

When I first heard of Canada's Confederation Poets, I thought that the name meant that they were a group of poets who wrote around the time of Canada's confederation of 1867. I checked out some of their poems and thought, well, they were not much worse than a lot of British Empire poets writing a half century after the late English Romantics. Imagine my surprise when I heard that the name referred to the time of their births, that some of their poems were written during the twentieth century! One of them, William Wilfred Campbell, wrote that winter "hath touched these hills austere," leaving a world "wherein / Nor love nor life nor hope hath ever been." Campbell was born in the same year as was Harriet Monroe, who would become the founder of *Poetry* magazine and champion of the Modernists Pound, H.D. and Eliot. The Confederation Poets (and most Canadian painters), unlike the Modernists, spent most of their time presenting what the seasons did to trees and hillsides and forest brooks. Archibald Lampman was a better poet than the others (contrary to what anthologist Campbell thought). Some professors who should have known better dubbed him "The Canadian Keats." Yes, he was one of those who could not resist riming "life" with "strife," but even with the challenging rime scheme he forced upon himself, he wrote in "We Too Shall Sleep" an affective poem about his unfortunate son without harming the language overmuch. He should have avoided putting "quiet grave" so close to "earthly lot," but we will forgive him his few high-falutin' verb endings, won't we?

William Butler Yeats (1865–1939)

An Irish Airman Foresees His Death

I know that I shall meet my fate
Somewhere among the clouds above;
Those that I fight I do not hate,
Those that I guard I do not love;
My country is Kiltartan Cross,
My countrymen Kiltartan's poor,
No likely end could bring them loss
Or leave them happier than before.
Nor law, nor duty bade me fight,
Nor public men, nor cheering crowds,
A lonely impulse of delight
Drove to this tumult in the clouds;
I balanced all, brought all to mind,
The years to come seemed waste of breath,
A waste of breath the years behind
In balance with this life, this death.

Here's yet another poem that rimes "breath" with "death."
But Yeats was too good a poet to rime "life" with "strife."
Until the beginning of the twentieth century, human beings
could not fly, but must only envy the birds and angels and
gods, some sporting wings attached by wax. The invention
of airplanes made some dreamers think that humans were
approaching divinity, but fifteen years after Kitty Hawk,
flying machines were proving the pessimistic view of H.G.
Wells, being used in the clash of empires called the Great
War. We would have to wait for Hart Crane if we wanted
poetry that saw the dark side of industrial ambition in the
sky. Yeats lived during a time of terrible violence in Europe
and in his little island, and his readers know his abhorrence
of armed struggle. Here he presents an orderly progression
of four quatrains that offer a logical argument that neverthe-
less ends up in a mystery (very Yeatsian, that) — and maybe a
clue about the making of poetry or any beauty in the midst
of something terrible. The Irish airman is on the earth when
he prophesies his death. He does not fight, he says, out of
love or hate or duty, any of those war-poem standards. He
does not even share anything with the people of his home-
town. He's going up for excitement, for the splendid moment,
for the quick breath that is not wasted, the flight that is a
poem's making — or was.

Gertrude Stein (1874–1946)

The House Was Just Twinkling in the Moon Light

The house was just twinkling in the moon light,
And inside it twinkling with delight,
Is my baby bright.
Twinkling with delight in the house twinkling
with the moonlight,
Bless my baby bless my baby bright,
Bless my baby twinkling with delight,
In the house twinkling in the moon light,
Her hubby dear loves to cheer when he thinks
and he always thinks when he knows and he always
knows that his blessed baby wifey is all here and he
is all hers, and sticks to her like burrs, blessed baby

Of course we know that this is a traditional love poem because it invokes or at least mentions the moon or at least its light. It is, further, a found poem, not in the usual sense of that term, i.e., a poem that was embedded, perhaps accidentally, in some other use of words, such as a government announcement. In this case it was one of the many love notes left by Gertrude Stein after a night's work on some other writing, to be found by Stein's "wifey" Alice B. Toklas, who woke each day to begin *her* work, the typing of the writing that Stein had done in the late night and early morning. You might consider these discoveries to follow a tradition that includes the poems that Queen Elizabeth I wrote on the walls and windows of her "prison" residence, and the little poem that William Carlos Williams left in the icebox to apologize to *his* wife for eating the delicious plums she had been saving for breakfast. It is hard to read Stein's poem without vocalizing, isn't it? And when you do, you come upon her famous repetition that is not really repetition, as Stein said more than once, because the second time the poem says "thinks" it is in the act of echoing the first time it said "thinks," and this in the context of all that "twinkling." You do see, don't you, or rather you do hear. Or rather you, like the blessed baby, hear the baby talk that is love talk whether "here" or "hers."

Robert Frost (1874–1963)

Stopping by Woods on a Snowy Evening

Whose woods these are I think I know.
His house is in the village though;
He will not see me stopping here
To watch his woods fill up with snow.

My little horse must think it queer
To stop without a farmhouse near
Between the woods and frozen lake
The darkest evening of the year.

He gives his harness bells a shake
To ask if there is some mistake.
The only other sound's the sweep
Of easy wind and downy flake.

The woods are lovely, dark and deep,
But I have promises to keep,
And miles to go before I sleep,
And miles to go before I sleep.

The first place I ever read this item was in a *Saturday Review* article in which John Ciardi praised it as a great U.S. poem. I was a neophyte, so I could not understand why squares in the academy thought so highly of Robert Frost. I'd always thought he was a sort of grandma, writing self-satisfied poems with a life's lesson at the end. Good fences make good neighbours. One could do worse than be a swinger of birches. Here we have a poem full of homey symbols to tell us that while death can be tempting at times such as the darkest evening of the year, one is supposed to ride on along what the Hallmark cards call life's journey. Of course the thing you notice first here is the poem's da dum da dum da dum da dum. You have heard it before, in Housman's poem about getting hammered on beer and sleeping it off in the mud. But Housman's da dum da dum is the frame on which a comic verse is hung. I don't think we are invited to say, "Oh, Robert, this is stupid stuff." Housman was not pretending to solemnity, so he was happy with his country couplets. Frost dares to remind us of the serious aim in Dante's epic, by adding a little extra to the great poet's *terza rima*. Maybe that reach for seriousness is the reason for inverting the syntax in the poem's first line. Or maybe it just fits the da dum better. Anyway, is Frost paying total attention, this person who can hear snow falling? Though the title and the first two stanzas mention stopping, the poem, if not the pony, keeps clopping on.

Ezra Pound (1885–1972)

A Pact

I make truce with you, Walt Whitman —
I have detested you long enough.
I come to you as a grown child
Who has had a pig-headed father;
I am old enough now to make friends.
It was you that broke the new wood,
Now is a time for carving.
We have one sap and one root —
Let there be commerce between us.

There are still some people who might tell you that this little poem "doesn't rhyme." These people, you could say, have their ears turned off. When we hear "detested," don't we hear "truce" again? Isn't it by ear that we get from "enough" to "father," back to "enough," and on to "friends"? And doesn't "make friends" chime with "make truce"? Or if we are remembering that sentence structure produces rime, don't we notice that the first three lines say "I" [vowel]? While we are at it, we might notice that this "grown child" is offering a truce in which compromise is suggested — grown child and stubborn father already share one sap and one root, but there will be something *between* them (note that root of two). Here we have a pretty good characterization of poetry's career, of a large work carried on by numerous workers. Ezra Pound was a poet who always maintained that sense of structure. You will find ancient language in his modernism — "o'er scant-logged ingle blaze" — soon to be followed by contemporary British or U.S. American slang, sometimes boisterous insults. You will also find multiple languages and histories that tell you that Pound's poetry, especially *The Cantos*, takes the whole world of all recorded time as its purview. Yet, listen to this poem, "A Pact" — in 1916 it fell upon ears that were used to melodious verse, inversions and convolutions and avoidances. Readers must have been jolted by the frank diction. Their forebears had been jolted by Walt Whitman. It would happen again.

H.D. (1886–1961)

Oread

Whirl up, sea —
Whirl your pointed pines,
Splash your great pines
On our rocks,
Hurl your green over us —
Cover us with your pools of fir.

This is my favourite Imagist poem. But if you were to remove its images and recite it with sounds only, you would get a lot of what the poem is "about." Try it. The poem comprises six short lines, and five of them begin with imperative verbs. If you take your time before each line, you can almost hear and therefore see the sea in waves crashing against the rocks at its edge. It must be a constant action, as the last word of the last line rimes with the first word of the first line. There is, in fact, a lot of rime going on: "whirl" rimes with another "whirl," and then with "hurl," before calming down with "fir." There is also a lot of front rime for such a short poem, the "pointed pines" touching lightly (like a smaller wave) on the second letter of "splash" before reappearing in "pines," then resting calmly in those "pools." But there is subtlety here, as the phoneme "r" (which in English is not a consonant) comes to us quietly thirteen times in twenty-six short words. One could go on, even though the poem is over so quickly, noticing that the letter "c" (hmm, sea) turns "over us" into "cover us." All right, but isn't there a lot to be said about the way H.D. titles the poem after the nymph that we associate with conifer forests, then addresses the sea (where one might expect nereids), then offers an image of large seagoing conifers, then asks (as a plural) to be inundated by "pools of fir"? And the first question I then asked was — who is "us"?

Margaret Avison (1918–2007)

The Hid, Here

Big birds fly past the window
trailing strings or vines
out in the big blue.

Big trees become designs
of delicate floral tracery
in golden green.

The Milky Way
end over end like a football
lobs, towards that still
unreachable elsewhere
that is hid within bud and nest-stuff and bright air
where the big birds flew
past the now waiting window.

I imagine that the first question one will have is: why "hid" instead of "hidden"? Maybe we are being encouraged to focus on sound instead of syntax, or we are being thrown there. What is it about "hid"? Well, it has what your teachers called a short eye, a vowel that will show up eighteen times in the twelve short lines and one longer one. (Does that numbering make this a sonnet? Is that what is hid?) (Well, it is an upside-down sonnet, with the demands of end-rime made on one occasion by colours. Neat.) If we look at the letter "i" instead of hearing its sounds, we see twenty-five of them. Maybe the subjective "I" is hid, then. You reply that it's the still (unmoving) unreachable elsewhere that is hid not so much beyond our galaxy but inside unseen spring stuff? This is fun. It is Avison at her ferreting, ideating, religious most usual. And of course, while we listen, she lets the syntax do its work on the poem and us. In the beginning, in the sestet where an octave is supposed to start us, big birds fly in the present continuous tense, and in the bottom of the octave they were in the past. There is a story not being fed to us, as we are not led, not to the hid. Try narrative, then: in the beginning of this upside-down poem, the big birds are busy making a nest for little birds, the littered nest that could at least be imagined were anyone looking through the waiting window. But that football? Is it not the opposite of hid, the way it sticks out? That fall thing?

Afterword

How to Enjoy a Good Evening Poem

Here is the way this project began. A few years ago my wife, Jean Baird, invented a new social-literary evening. For years we had been hosting a book club, and for as many years we had been hosting potluck dinners. Why don't we, she suggested, have meetings at which we discuss single poems instead of books, and at the same gatherings have potlucks, in which the food illustrates in some manner the poem of the evening?

So we did. First I would choose a one-page poem. Then Jean would send it via email to all our members. You can imagine an ingredient pertinent to Blake's "Ah Sun-flower!" Yes, someone brought a bottle of Al Purdy's wild grape wine to Emerson's "Concord Hymn." The New Brunswick genius David Farwell had to perform some complicated argument for coming to every meeting with his reportedly famous meat loaf.

But my favourite dish, or call it feat, was carried off and carried in by the novelist Kevin Chong. Taking John Keats's grave marker at the Protestant graveyard just outside Rome's ancient wall as his inspiration, Kevin presented a big gravestone-shaped block of jelly the colour of water, into the surface of which were inserted the black jelly letters KEATS.

You might want to do something like that, or you might want to get yourself a lined notebook and do what I did — write a page in response to each of the poems in this little book.

Index of First Lines

George Bowering approaches literature as he does life: with a playful gravity and a grave merriness that makes intellectual life and writing seem at once attractive, unintimidating and remarkable. He dispels the myth of literature being hard or tricky, and demonstrates, as he reads and chats, the accessible and enriching nature of great literature. Born in the Okanagan Valley, Bowering has taught literature and writing at the University of Calgary, the University of Western Ontario, Simon Fraser University and others. Bowering won the Governor General's Award for poetry in 1969 and fiction in 1980. In 2002 he was made the first ever Canadian Parlimentary Poet Laureate. He lives in Vancouver with his wife Jean.

In 2017, to honour NeWest Press' 40th anniversary, we inaug-
urated a new poetry series to go alongside our Nunatak First
Fiction, Prairie Play, and Writer as Critic series: Crow Said
Poetry. Crow Said is named in honour of Robert Kroetsch's
foundational 1977 novel *What The Crow Said*. The series
aims to shed light on places and people outside of the literary
mainstream. It is our intention that the poets featured in this
series will continue Robert Kroetsch's literary tradition of
innovation, interrogation, and generosity of spirit.